Contents

1: The Facts About HIV/AIDS

Most people have now heard of the terrible disease known as AIDS, and are familiar with the term 'HIV positive', yet only a few decades ago this infection was almost unknown. Back in the early 1980s, not even doctors and scientists knew that a global disaster was about to strike.

Today, AIDS is one of the biggest health problems facing the world. At the end of 2002, 42 million people worldwide were thought to be infected with the virus which causes AIDS. And it is increasingly becoming a disease of the young – around half of all new cases are in teenagers and young people. Yet AIDS is a preventable disease. If everyone knew how the infection was spread, and how to keep themselves safe, it would eventually become a thing of the past.

The free and easy nightlife of American cities allowed HIV to spread quickly in the 1980s.

21st CENTURY CITIZEN
AIDS

Kristina Routh

FRANKLIN WATTS

Titles in this series:
AIDS
Animal Rights
Genetic Engineering
Immigrants and Refugees
Terrorism
World Hunger

© 2004 Arcturus Publishing Ltd

Produced for Franklin Watts by
Arcturus Publishing Ltd, 26/27 Bickels Yard,
151-153 Bermondsey Street, London SE1 3HA.

Series concept: Alex Woolf
Project editor: Kelly Davis
Designer: Stonecastle Graphics
Consultant: Kaye Stearman
Picture researcher: Shelley Noronha,
    Glass Onion Pictures

Published in the UK by Franklin Watts.

British Library Cataloguing Publication Data
A CIP catalogue record for this book is
available from the British Library.

ISBN 0 7496 5461 9

Printed and bound in Italy

Franklin Watts – the Watts Publishing Group,
96 Leonard Street, London EC2A 4XD.

Picture acknowledgements
GlaxoSmithKline 38; National AIDS Trust, UK,
16, 44; Photofusion cover (Steve Eason) below
and 43, 10 (Ray Roberts), 15 (Brian Mitchell), 21
(Brenda Prince), 31 (Paul Baldesare), 45 (Mo
Wilson); Popperfoto cover (Howard Burditt)
above and 32, 1 and 40 (Antony Njuguna), 9
(Heinz-Peter Bader), 11 (Gustau Nacarino), 20
(Kim Ulish), 22 (Guang Niu), 23 (Denis
Balibouse), 39 (George Mulala), 34 (Peter
Andrews), 36 (Mike Hutchings), 37 (Dima
Korotayev), 38/39 (Albert Gea), 41 (Rafiqur
Rahman), 42 (Kevin Lamarque); Science Photo
Library 6 (National Institute of Allergies and
Infectious Diseases), 12 (CNRI), 24, 25 (Jim
Olive, Peter Arnold Inc.), 26 and 29 (John Cole);
Skjold Photographs 18, 28; Topham 4 (David
Wells), 7, 19, 30, 33 (Adil Bradlow);
WHO/UNAIDS 8.

Cover pictures: Care supporter visits people living with AIDS in Zambia (above). Crowds attend AIDS vigil on World AIDS Day (below).

Note to parents and teachers
Some recommended websites are listed under 'Useful Addresses' at the back of this book. Every effort has been made by the Publishers to ensure that these websites are suitable for children; that they are of the highest educational value; and that they contain no inappropriate or offensive material. However, because of the nature of the Internet, it is impossible to guarantee that the contents of these sites will not be altered. We strongly advise that Internet access is supervised by a responsible adult.

PERSPECTIVES

'HIV/AIDS has dramatically and devastatingly affected the lives of millions of people living with the disease, their families, children, communities and countries.'

The Sexuality Information and Education Council of the United States, 2002

What do the terms 'AIDS' and 'HIV' mean?

People use the term 'AIDS' because it is quick and easy to say, but the full name of this disease is 'Acquired Immune Deficiency Syndrome'. Someone with AIDS has a collection of signs or symptoms (a 'syndrome') caused by damage to the immune system (the body's defences against invading micro-organisms). This is described as 'immune deficiency'. The term 'acquired' is just a way of saying that someone catches it, rather than it being a problem he or she has always had.

HIV is the Human Immunodeficiency Virus, the tiny micro-organism which eventually causes AIDS. Someone may be infected with this virus for many years without any problems but at some point he or she will start to become severely ill. All the evidence shows that once a person is infected with HIV (known as being 'HIV positive') he or she will always be infected.

AIDS is the last stage of HIV infection, so it makes sense to talk about these two ideas together. Because of this, the term 'HIV/AIDS' will often be used in this book.

In the beginning

In 1981, doctors in New York saw eight young men with a rare form of skin cancer, Kaposi's sarcoma. They were very surprised because this condition usually only affected elderly men. At about the same time, other doctors in New York and California were faced with an unusually large number of patients showing signs of a rare lung infection, Pneumocystis carinii pneumonia (PCP). Strangely, these patients were also all young men and, like those with Kaposi's sarcoma, all were gay (homosexual). The doctors did not realize it but they were seeing the first cases of AIDS, and these few patients were soon to be followed by many more.

Although HIV/AIDS appeared to begin in the USA in the early 1980s, the disease had been around for a lot longer. Looking at blood samples taken decades earlier, scientists later found a case of HIV infection in Africa from as early as the 1950s. However, it was probably not until the late 1970s that the disease really began to spread.

No one yet knew what to call this strange new disease. It was given various names, both by the doctors treating it and by the newspapers reporting it. Eventually, in mid-1982, the term AIDS began to be widely used.

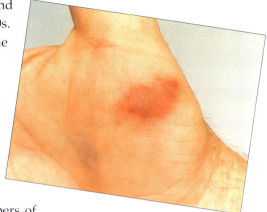

The hand of a person with AIDS, showing Kaposi's sarcoma on the palm.

The blood connection

At first, many people thought AIDS only affected members of the gay community. Then others started to show signs of the disease. People with haemophilia, a disorder of the blood, treated with Factor VIII, a human blood product, began to become ill. Individuals who shared bloodstained needles to inject themselves with illegal drugs started to show symptoms of AIDS. And in late 1982 a baby died of AIDS after being given a blood transfusion.

Obviously, whatever caused AIDS could be passed on through blood or blood products, and this made people scared. Newspapers started to produce articles with headlines about 'Killer Blood', and many people became too afraid to donate blood. They thought, wrongly, that they might catch AIDS that way.

The AIDS explosion

After the first cases of AIDS in the USA in 1981, the numbers began to increase dramatically, both in the USA and elsewhere. By the end of 1983, American doctors had seen 3,000 cases. Only

PERSPECTIVES

Palle, a boy with haemophilia from Denmark, was ten years old when he was diagnosed with HIV infection.

'I clearly remember the day when my father told me that I had contracted HIV. I didn't understand much of it. I had no idea how serious that was.'

Danish newspaper article, author Susanne Lundbeck, October 1992

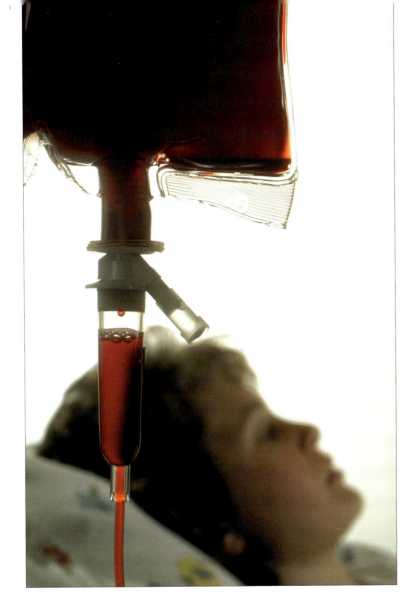

A patient receiving a blood transfusion in hospital. Some people were infected with HIV by blood transfusions in the 1980s. However this is now very rare because most countries test blood for HIV infection before using it.

four years later, in 1987, the number had risen to 47,000. Countries in Europe were also seeing alarming rises in the numbers of people showing the symptoms of AIDS. At the end of 1984, there were 762 reported cases of AIDS in Europe. Two years later, there had been a fivefold increase – to 3,800. Elsewhere in the world, AIDS was spreading. However, in many developing countries, such as parts of Africa, the healthcare system was not advanced enough for AIDS to be diagnosed.

The World Health Organization (WHO), the international body which monitors the health of people all over the world, began to collect figures on AIDS cases in 1983. At that time, around 28 countries had reported cases. Three years later, AIDS had appeared in 85 countries all across the world. By 1987, the WHO estimated that 10 million people worldwide had been infected with HIV.

PERSPECTIVES

'In many parts of the world there is anxiety, bafflement, a sense that something has to be done – although no one knows what'.

The New York Times, *1983*

This rapid explosion continued into the 1990s, with the biggest increases in parts of Africa. By the end of 1996, HIV/AIDS was thought to have infected 23 million people around the world, and killed nearly 6.5 million.

As the twenty-first century dawned, the disease continued to spread. Nowadays, while many developed countries seem to be bringing it under control, some developing countries with huge populations (such as India), and the former Soviet Union in Eastern Europe, are moving towards their own HIV/AIDS explosions. In parts of Africa, particularly the South and East, HIV/AIDS has caused real devastation. By the end of 2001, there were more than 11 million orphans in Africa due to HIV/AIDS.

All in all, the HIV/AIDS situation now looks very serious. In 2002, there were 5 million new cases of HIV infection, and 3 million deaths due to AIDS. This number will probably keep increasing unless something can be done to stop it.

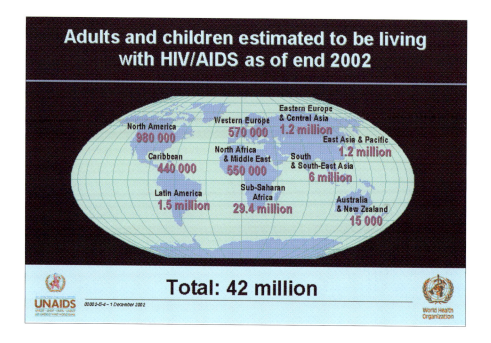

Where did the virus come from?

One of the great mysteries about HIV/AIDS is where exactly it came from. There have been many theories, including the idea that the virus was manufactured as a kind of secret biological weapon! In fact the most likely explanation is that HIV might have developed from a similar virus which was infecting our nearest relatives, chimpanzees, in West Africa.

The relatively rapid spread of the virus across the world in the 1980s has been put down to a number of factors, including the use of blood transfusions and blood products, and the great rise in the abuse of illegal drugs and needle sharing. Increased air travel, by allowing large numbers of people to travel long distances relatively easily, has also helped the spread of infectious diseases like HIV.

Who discovered the AIDS virus?

In May 1983, doctors at the Institute Pasteur in France reported that they had found a new virus which they believed to be the cause of AIDS. They called it lymphadenopathy associated virus (LAV). In April 1984, an American, Dr Robert Gallo of the National Cancer Institute, announced that his team had discovered the AIDS virus. They named their virus HTLV-III. The following year, these two viruses were shown to be the same organism. This virus was later renamed HIV, the Human Immunodeficiency Virus.

Dr Robert Gallo, one of the first people to identify the virus that causes AIDS.

An argument sprang up between the French researchers and the American scientists, as each claimed to have discovered the virus first. The matter was finally decided after the French scientists began a court case in 1985. It was finally agreed, out of court, that both groups would share the discovery.

PERSPECTIVES

'The origin of AIDS remains steeped in controversy.'

Chris Fritzen, AIDS Project Los Angeles, 2000

How HIV is spread

When someone is infected with HIV the virus is present in certain body fluids: blood, semen, vaginal secretions and breast milk. The only way the infection can be passed on is if one or more of these fluids passes from an infected person into another person's body.

This means there are several main ways of spreading HIV infection, sometimes known as 'high-risk activities':

- During unprotected sex, including vaginal, anal and oral sex. 'Unprotected' means that no steps have been taken to avoid HIV infection, such as wearing a condom. This is the most common way that HIV infection is spread.
- By sharing needles for intravenous drug abuse – 'shooting up'. When a needle is used, a small amount of blood may be sucked up into the needle or syringe. This may then be injected into the next person who uses the needle.
- During pregnancy, childbirth or breastfeeding, when the mother is infected with HIV and passes it on to her child.
- Via a blood transfusion or blood products. This is now very rare, as, in many countries, all blood is tested for HIV infection before it is used.

...and how it is *not* spread

Many people are scared of having any contact with people who are infected with HIV, so it is important to know how the virus is not spread. HIV is not passed on through coughing, sneezing, touching, hugging, kissing, sharing kitchen utensils or bathroom facilities. There is no threat from mosquitoes or other biting insects because the amount of blood they may pass on is too small to cause infection. It is, in fact, extremely unlikely that people will catch HIV unless they engage in one of the high-risk activities listed above.

An HIV information poster produced for schools.

A drug addict drops used syringes into a container in Barcelona, Spain. Needle exchange programmes can help stop the spread of HIV/AIDS infection.

Preventing spread

For most people, preventing HIV/AIDS is a matter of avoiding high-risk activities. Prevention advice includes:

- Abstinence, which means no sexual activity at all. This is the message many feel is right to give to young people: that they should wait until they are old enough to form lasting relationships before they start having sex.

- 'Safe sex', which means sexual contact with a partner where there is no exchange of semen, vaginal fluids or blood. If sexual intercourse takes place, a condom should be worn. The lower the number of sexual partners, the lower the risk of catching HIV.

- Not injecting intravenous drugs, or never sharing needles with others. In some areas the authorities provide 'needle exchanges' where clean needles are given to addicts who just cannot give up.

CASE STUDY

Clint was 17 when he discovered he had become infected with HIV. He had been in a relationship for only a short time but had not used a condom during sex. He says, 'I didn't know anything about HIV.'

His mum was with Clint when the doctor told him his blood tests showed he was HIV positive. He remembers, 'That was what hurt me the most, to see my mum in pain.' Clint was quite sick for a while but now feels great, although he has to take 15 pills a day.

Clint has since set up a charity to help and support other young people like himself. He says, 'When I tested positive there was no support group. I couldn't meet anyone similar to my age who was positive.' By learning about HIV and the way it spreads, he hopes other teenagers won't face the uncertain future that he does.

(Source: BBCi website, UK, 2003)

What does HIV/AIDS do to the body?

HIV makes someone ill by damaging their immune system. If the immune system is damaged, the body cannot fight off infections properly and the person keeps getting ill.

HIV affects one part of the immune system in particular – special cells called T-helper lymphocytes (also known as T-cells). In HIV infection, the virus enters the T-cells, then takes them over, making them produce lots of new copies of the virus. The cell then breaks apart and these new viruses can enter the bloodstream to infect more T-cells. This process repeats itself over and over again.

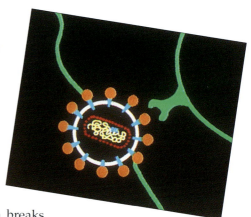

A T-cell infected with HIV (left) about to fuse with another, non-infected T-cell (right).

The stages of HIV infection

HIV infection can cause many different medical conditions, ranging from minor ailments such as skin rashes and nausea to severe life-threatening cancers and infections.

Generally the longer people are infected with HIV, the more seriously ill they become. When people are first infected they may just have a mild flu-like illness, or may not notice the infection at all. For some, there may then be a long period (even many years) when they remain quite well. This is called the 'asymptomatic stage'.

After a time, though, the HIV infection causes so much damage to the body's immune system that it can no longer cope. Health problems that would normally be prevented by the immune system, such as some unusual infections and cancers, may then start to appear.

The most extreme illnesses occur in the final stage of HIV infection, AIDS. Although, with treatment, people can manage and even survive many of these illnesses, as far as we know the HIV virus will never leave the body, and people with HIV will always be at risk of developing full-blown AIDS.

Acute HIV infection – the first few weeks
- No symptoms at all.
- Mild 'flu'-like illness: fever, sweats, chills, swollen lymph glands, skin rashes

Early symptoms of HIV infection (possibly after years of being symptom-free)
- Thrush: a fungal condition, very common in HIV infection. White patches on the inside of the mouth and tongue; a burning sensation and altered sense of taste.
- Shingles: caused by the chicken pox virus, which reappears when immunity is low. Causes a red, blistering skin rash. Can be very painful.
- Herpes simplex: a common viral infection, which can be sexually transmitted. Causes a blistering skin rash.

Later stages including the severe late stage, AIDS
- Pneumocystis pneumonia: a severe lung infection caused by the parasite *Pneumocystis pneumoniae*. Very common in AIDS, it causes breathlessness, dry cough and fever.
- Kaposi's sarcoma: an unusual skin cancer which can also affect the internal organs. Appears as brownish or purple skin patches.
- Nervous system effects: mental confusion, forgetfulness and even dementia (loss of the ability to think and reason). Blindness may occur.
- Tuberculosis: a serious and long-lasting bacterial infection, which damages the lungs and other parts of the body. Causes fever, cough and weight loss.

General symptoms of HIV infection
These may be present at all times but become increasingly severe in the later stages of HIV infection. These are partly due to the HIV infection itself, partly to the other illnesses that may accompany it.
- Weight loss and fatigue
- Diarrhoea and fever

DEBATE
If you discovered a friend had HIV/AIDS, would you want to be around them any more? Would you be afraid of catching HIV/AIDS yourself?

2: Attitudes Towards HIV/AIDS

One of the biggest problems for those who have HIV/AIDS is the way they are treated by other people. Across the world, they have been excluded, feared, punished and even killed. Many have lost their jobs, their homes and even their families. This is because, in many countries, the disease carries a stigma, meaning that it is considered shameful to have HIV/AIDS. Understandably, people with HIV/AIDS may therefore be too scared to tell others that they have it, for fear of what might happen to them.

There are several reasons why HIV/AIDS carries such a stigma. One is because of its links with sex, and in particular with homosexuality (since HIV/AIDS first appeared in the developed world in homosexual men, and some people consider homosexuality to be morally wrong). In the same way, the link with drug abuse means that those with HIV/AIDS may be thought to have acted irresponsibly and even illegally.

Stigma is also caused by fear and ignorance. A fatal disease, which can be passed from person to person, is bound to cause fear. And if people do not understand exactly how it is passed on, they will almost certainly be afraid of those who have it. In the past, some people with cancer (another disease that can be fatal) also used to find themselves feared and isolated, and would often hide the truth about their condition. As the general public has become more informed about cancer, this stigma has lessened. Perhaps one day the stigma of HIV/AIDS will be removed in a similar way.

PERSPECTIVES

'If HIV-related stigma and discrimination are not tackled, AIDS will blight the 21st century just as racism affected the 20th century.'

Dr Peter Piot, Executive Director of the Joint United Nations Programme on HIV/AIDS (UNAIDS), 2001

PERSPECTIVES

'Having HIV is a stigma which makes it impossible for people like me to live a life without lying...'

23-year-old man from Australia, HIV/AIDS Positive Stories website, 2003

Why does it matter what people think?

It matters for individuals. It is hard enough for people with HIV/AIDS to cope with their medical problems without being faced with additional social difficulties. Families and friends may find it shocking that their loved ones have HIV/AIDS, employers may make it difficult for them to keep their jobs or get new ones, and neighbours may begin to avoid them. Because of their fears about the way they will be treated, many people decide not to get tested for HIV/AIDS, or keep the diagnosis to themselves. This can lead to problems in seeking proper treatment.

Being excluded from a group can be very painful.

It also matters for society. Because of the stigma, people convince themselves that HIV/AIDS is something which happens to 'other' people who bring it upon themselves. This attitude makes it difficult for society to teach them the facts about HIV/AIDS and how to keep themselves safe, and may lead to problems in

WHEN YOU'RE HIV POSITIVE, YOU GET USED TO PEOPLE LOOKING STRAIGHT THROUGH YOU.

ARE YOU HIV PREJUDICED?

A poster from the 'Are you HIV prejudiced?' campaign, used on shop windows.

PERSPECTIVES

'Discrimination against people living with HIV/AIDS, or those thought to be infected, is a clear violation of their human rights.'

The Joint United Nations Programme on HIV/AIDS (UNAIDS), fact sheet on discrimination

PERSPECTIVES

An anonymous contributor to the Queensland Positive People website, Australia, has this to say (she and her husband are both infected):

'My biggest hope is that my children will one day be able to talk about this, the way their daddy died or the illness their mummy has, without feeling ashamed or embarrassed. HIV can affect anybody. We all are everyday people living everyday lives.'

preventing spread of the virus. It also means that society may not accept responsibility for the care of people with HIV/AIDS. In the worst situations it leads to whole sections of society, such as the gay community, being treated unkindly because of their links with HIV/AIDS.

Fighting the stigma

But much is being done to improve this situation. The importance of treating people with HIV/AIDS fairly was demonstrated by the choice of the theme 'Stigma and Discrimination' for World AIDS Day in 2003. One group in the UK, the National AIDS Trust, launched a national two-week campaign in 2003 called 'Are you HIV prejudiced?'. This campaign used advertisements on the radio, in newspapers and on the Internet to send the Trust's message to a wide audience, including young people.

AIDS – discrimination and human rights

Many countries have laws to stop people being treated unfairly because of their skin colour, religion, sex or disability. These are called anti-discrimination laws and they show that the people of that country believe that all human beings have certain rights which must be protected. The Universal Declaration of Human Rights, agreed by the many countries of the United Nations in 1948, lists many of these rights.

According to anti-discrimination laws, people should not be treated badly just because they have a particular medical condition. Individuals with HIV/AIDS therefore have the right to be treated fairly. They should not be stopped from getting jobs, sacked from the jobs they do have, excluded from proper healthcare, or treated in any way differently just because of their condition.

CASE STUDY

The Ray brothers – Ricky, Robby and Randy – lived with their parents in the small town of Arcadia, Florida, during the early 1980s. The boys were just normal kids, except that they each had haemophilia, an inherited blood disease. Unfortunately, like many others who received treatment for this condition with Factor VIII, a blood product, they became infected with HIV.

People in the town became scared. In 1986, when the boys were aged nine, eight and seven, they were banned from school because of fears that they might spread the virus to other children. The local pastor asked them not to come to church. When a federal judge ordered the school to take them back, many parents kept their children at home, and the Rays' house was doused with gasoline and set alight.

Eventually, unable to live in the community any longer, the family moved away to start a new life.

Mrs Ray with two of her sons.

Guilty or innocent?

A 1998 survey conducted by the National Institute of Mental Health in the USA found that nearly one-third of Americans believed that if people had become infected with HIV/AIDS through sex or drug use then they had 'got what they deserved'. This showed that, in the minds of many people, those with HIV/AIDS are divided into two groups: the 'guilty' and the 'innocent'.

Those who have caught HIV/AIDS through unprotected sex, especially gay sex, and intravenous drug abuse, have been seen by many as being guilty ('having only themselves to blame'), while those who were infected by, for instance, a blood transfusion or the use of blood products are seen as 'innocent victims'. But many believe this distinction is unfair, and feel that it has only increased the difficulties facing people who are living with HIV/AIDS today.

AIDS and the media

From the early 1980s onwards, the media has played a powerful role in the HIV/AIDS story. There have been reports on the disease in newspapers, on the radio and television, and later on the Internet. Some of these reports have been very negative and inaccurate, and have caused a great deal of harm. Others have been both helpful and informative, providing a vital weapon in the fight against HIV/AIDS.

Most newspapers, radio stations and TV channels exist to make money and they therefore tend to report things in a way that is likely to attract a large audience. This may often mean that they reflect people's fear and ignorance about HIV/AIDS. It was, for instance, in the newspapers that the unpleasant term 'Gay Plague' was first used for AIDS, and there have been many headlines including the words 'Killer Disease'. People with HIV/AIDS have often been portrayed as irresponsible, immoral and dangerous.

Yet careful reporting of the facts about this disease in all aspects of the media has also helped people learn about the real risks of HIV/AIDS. Television has been used particularly well, with examples such as the 'AIDS Week' in February 1987 in the UK where many different programmes were shown on all aspects of the subject. Well-known personalities like 'Magic' Johnson, the American basketball player with HIV/AIDS, used the media to tell the world their stories and help educate others.

Tom Hanks in *Philadelphia*.

Many good storylines about HIV/AIDS have appeared in television programmes, books and movies. In the 1993 movie *Philadelphia*, well-known actor Tom Hanks played a young man with HIV/AIDS and was able to put a human face on the disease. Sympathetic stories like this have done much to help people see that HIV/AIDS can happen to anyone, and that those with the condition are not to be feared but supported.

CASE STUDY

Earvin 'Magic' Johnson was one of America's most dazzling basketball players when, in November 1991, he shocked his fans by announcing his retirement. He was HIV positive.

This announcement caused great excitement in the media, and also among those who were campaigning in the field of HIV/AIDS. Here was a famous, well-loved man who was prepared to stand up and admit he had the disease that everyone was so frightened of. People began talking more openly about HIV and many who had it themselves found that their lives became a little easier.

Years later, supported by anti-HIV medicines, Magic Johnson is still healthy and says, 'I feel wonderful. I celebrate life and I live every day. Every day is a holiday for me!'

(Source: USA Today website, 2001)

Media campaigns across the world

Using television, radio, newspapers and, increasingly, the Internet, health charities and government organizations are broadcasting the message about HIV/AIDS to millions of people.

One such campaign was that by the French medical charity Médecins sans Frontières ('Doctors without Borders'), in the Ukraine in Eastern Europe in 2001. Through television and radio commercials, distribution of leaflets and posters, advertisements and a website, the campaign aimed to inform the Ukrainian

Magic Johnson came out of retirement to play basketball for the Los Angeles Lakers in California in 1996, five years after he had been diagnosed HIV positive.

people of the true facts about HIV and AIDS and to reduce discrimination against those who had it.

The problem of prevention

It should be quite simple to stop the spread of HIV/AIDS since there are only a few ways in which it can be passed on. So why are people still becoming infected?

The main problem is that HIV/AIDS is linked with sex, which, in many societies, is a difficult subject to talk about. Teaching people how to keep themselves safe from HIV infection involves discussing sex and sexuality in a very frank way. Many adults are afraid that if they speak to young people about sex and condoms this will encourage them to start having sexual relationships before they are really old enough. In some countries, sometimes for cultural reasons, sex cannot be spoken about openly at all.

Even if people know that using a condom is the best way to guard against catching HIV during sex, they may still not use one. Sometimes this is due to embarrassment between partners, or the idea that 'it won't happen to me'. And some individuals might feel they would be viewed with suspicion if they insisted on a condom being worn. This unwillingness to speak freely about sex makes it very difficult to give people the information they need to make safe choices.

Many parents find it difficult to discuss sexual issues with their children.

PERSPECTIVES

'HIV/AIDS is a global emergency claiming 8000 lives a day in some of the poorest countries of the world. The Stop AIDS campaign is working to end this.'

UK Consortium on AIDS and International Development, 2002

Another big problem is that there are many people who have the virus but do not realize it. A person can be infected for many years without having symptoms and so may have had no reason to be tested for HIV. Although the infected person is not sick he or she can still pass on the infection to others. This situation is made worse by the stigma associated with HIV/AIDS which means that many people are too frightened to get an HIV test; they would rather not know.

Government attitudes to HIV/AIDS

The way the leader of a country views HIV/AIDS has a great impact on the chances of it being controlled there. Government attitudes vary a great deal. Many accept the facts about the dangers of HIV/AIDS and work hard to combat the disease within their countries and elsewhere. These include the governments of most developed countries such as the USA and UK, along with some developing nations such as Uganda in Africa. Unfortunately other governments, including that of Russia, find it harder to accept that their people might be at risk and seem to ignore the problem, while the rates of HIV/AIDS

A Chinese man donates his blood at an official mobile blood-collecting centre in Beijing in 2000. China has no national blood-screening programme, and the United Nations has predicted that it could have 10 million or more HIV/AIDS sufferers by 2010.

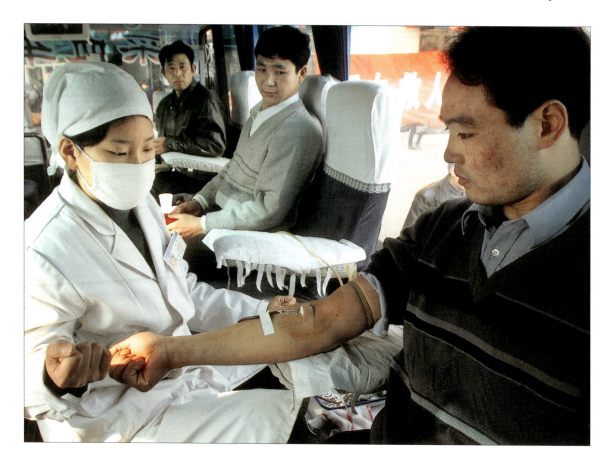

climb ever higher in their countries. In China, the rates of HIV infection are treated almost as a state secret, with government officials making it difficult for any outside organizations to help. And at least one country, South Africa, has some leaders who have denied that AIDS is due to HIV infection at all!

AIDS denial

Some people do not believe that AIDS is caused by HIV infection. This is called 'AIDS denial'. These people, sometimes known as 'AIDS dissidents', say that the disease we know as AIDS is actually a collection of diseases which have different causes, such as poverty, poor nutrition and even anti-AIDS medicines. They say it is a coincidence that people with AIDS are also infected with HIV.

One of the most well-known AIDS dissidents is the South African President Thabo Mbeki, who has made public statements supporting this view. However, the great majority of scientists all over the world are convinced that there is enough evidence to say that HIV does indeed cause AIDS. In July 1999, over 5,000 scientists from 82 countries signed a long and detailed statement to this effect, known as the 'Durban Declaration' (named after Durban, South Africa). It included the comment: 'HIV causes AIDS. It is unfortunate that a few vocal people deny the evidence. This position will cost countless lives'.

South African President Thabo Mbeki, at a news conference in 2003.

In August 2003, the South African government finally gave in to public pressure and made plans for the widespread use of anti-HIV medicines to treat their people with HIV/AIDS.

DEBATE

If someone says they have HIV/AIDS, is it right to ask them how they caught the virus? Would the answer affect how you behave towards them?

3: Living with HIV/AIDS

The only way to find out if a person is infected with HIV is to do a blood test. A doctor or nurse takes a small sample of blood, usually from the arm, and sends it to the laboratory for analysis.

When someone becomes infected with HIV his or her body begins to fight off the virus by making special chemicals called antibodies. The laboratory will look for these antibodies in the sample of blood they receive. If HIV antibodies are present the person is said to be 'HIV positive'; he or she has been infected with the virus. Even if such people feel well, they now know that they carry the virus and so can infect other people.

It can take around three months for the body to produce enough antibodies to be detected by the blood test. Sometimes it can be as long as six months. During this time, known as the 'window period', an infected person may have a negative HIV test, but will still be able to pass on the virus.

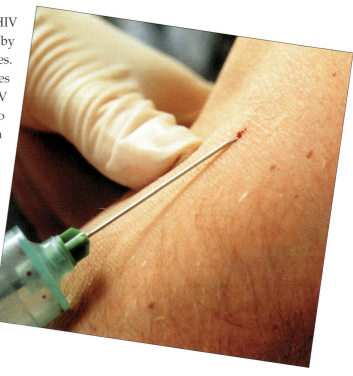

A nurse draws blood from a patient.

Deciding to have a test

Why do people have an HIV test? Some people are just worried and want to check that they are OK. Others may have had sex without using a condom, or have been sharing needles for drug-taking, and know they might be at risk. In many countries, including the USA and the UK, pregnant women are offered an HIV test along with their other routine blood tests.

No one should make the decision to have an HIV test without having the chance to discuss it with a trained counsellor. In nearly all cases, HIV testing is done anonymously. This means that the person who is tested can then make the decision about who he or she will tell. If people are HIV positive, there may be many changes in their lives.

Some may not want the test because they are afraid that they will be treated badly by others because of the stigma which surrounds HIV/AIDS. They may also find that having a positive test means that they have problems getting life or health insurance.

However, there are many good reasons to have the test:

- If it is negative, people can be reassured so they no longer have to worry.
- If it is positive, they can receive the right medical care.
- People who are positive will then know that they need to take extra precautions so as not to pass it on to someone else.
- If doctors know a pregnant woman is HIV positive, they can take steps that will greatly reduce the chances of the baby catching the infection.

A young man (left) receives one-to-one counselling at an HIV/AIDS clinic in Houston, Texas, USA.

Treatment for HIV/AIDS

There are no medicines yet which can completely cure someone of HIV infection. However, there are some which may stop an infected person from becoming ill for many years. Once started, these medicines have to be taken for the rest of that person's life.

The medicines used to treat HIV infection are known as anti-HIV medicines, 'antivirals' or sometimes 'antiretrovirals'. These work by stopping the virus from reproducing itself within the body. It is important that the infected person takes more than one of these medicines at a time. If only one medicine is taken, the virus can mutate (change) to become resistant to that medicine – which means that it no longer kills the virus. If two or more medicines are taken together, there is much less chance of this happening. Taking several medicines together is known as 'combination therapy', one form of which is HAART ('Highly Active Antiretroviral Therapy').

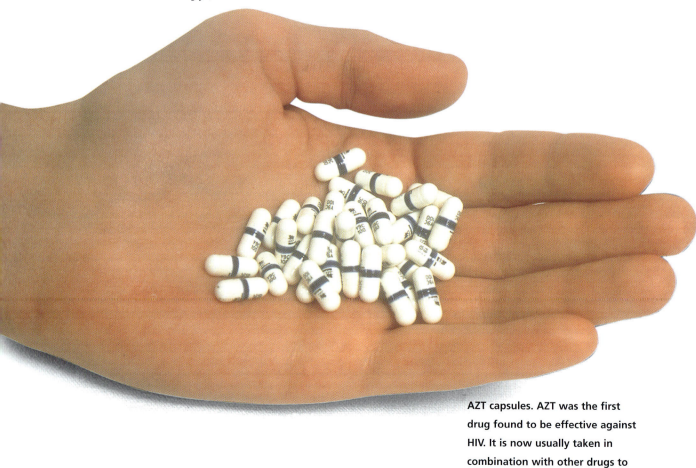

AZT capsules. AZT was the first drug found to be effective against HIV. It is now usually taken in combination with other drugs to prevent the virus developing resistance to it.

It can be quite difficult to take the medicines needed for HIV/AIDS. That is because there are so many of them, and they have to be taken at specific times. They can have some unpleasant side-effects as well, including vomiting and extreme tiredness. These medicines are also very expensive, which can be a major problem for those who live in countries without a free healthcare service. Someone who is on combination therapy needs to be very organized and highly motivated.

Anti-HIV medicines

The first type of antivirals used against HIV was introduced in 1987. They are known as 'reverse transcriptase inhibitors'. This long name just means that these medicines are able to inhibit, or block, a special chemical called 'reverse transcriptase' which the virus uses to make copies of itself. The most well-known of these medicines is AZT (also called Zidovudine or Retrovir).

Another, newer group of antivirals are known as 'protease inhibitors'. These, which have been used since 1995, stop the virus from reproducing itself. They do this by inhibiting another necessary chemical, 'protease'.

There are also other, newer, medicines on the way. Research is continually being carried out across the world to find safer, more effective medicines to fight HIV infection.

Other treatments

When people are infected with HIV/AIDS their immune systems are weakened. This makes them more likely to catch other infections which may make them very ill. However, unlike the HIV itself, these infections can often be completely cured with medicines such as antibiotics. Hospital treatment may also be needed in these situations.

PERSPECTIVES

'I am taking 25 pills a day. If I didn't have my family to keep me on medication, I wouldn't be alive right now.'

Nina, USA, from HIV Insite's teenage website

Care and support

Anyone who is ill needs care and support from those around them. This is certainly true of people with HIV/AIDS who may have a lot of problems to face. These problems will not only involve their health, but also the stigma and discrimination that the condition can arouse. For those with HIV/AIDS, support means finding guidance, strength and hope from people who are prepared to listen without judging.

Such support can come in many different ways, and from many different people. Most will turn to family and friends, but there are also trained HIV counsellors, support groups and various HIV/AIDS support services.

Family and friends can give wonderfully strong support to their loved one who has HIV/AIDS, but sometimes it can be very hard for that person to admit that he or she has been infected. Many people with HIV/AIDS fear that their family and friends may reject them if they know the truth. But hopefully, after the initial shock, families and friends will accept the situation, perhaps learning more about the condition themselves so that they can be supportive and understanding.

Sympathy and understanding are vital.

Counselling

Many people with HIV/AIDS, especially those who have just found out that they are infected, find it helpful to speak to an AIDS counsellor. Counsellors know all the facts about HIV/AIDS, and also know how best to support those who have it. This often means listening to people with HIV/AIDS, letting them express their feelings and fears about the condition in a place where they feel safe to do so. Sometimes people with HIV/AIDS may gather together in a small group, perhaps with a counsellor present, to share their feelings and support each other.

PERSPECTIVES

'Going to the support group was the first time I met other teenagers with AIDS. They looked like normal healthy teenagers. Through this group I learned to feel more comfortable with my AIDS status and realized that it wasn't my fault that I had AIDS.'

Kathryn, 20, USA, from 'The Body' website

AIDS support services

There are some government-run AIDS support services. There are also many different charities that have been formed to help increase understanding of the virus, and support those who are affected by it. These charities may provide telephone helplines, counsellors and drop-in centres for those with HIV/AIDS. Some of their addresses are listed at the end of this book.

Some organizations, such as The Body in the USA and the Terrence Higgins Trust in the UK, also provide help through the 'buddy system'. A buddy is a volunteer who befriends someone with AIDS, on a one-to-one basis, and helps him or her cope at this difficult time.

An HIV positive man and a volunteer 'buddy' at the London Lighthouse hospice, UK, which merged with the Terrence Higgins Trust in 2000.

Young people – a group at risk

Young people seem to be particularly at risk from HIV/AIDS. In mid-2002 it was estimated that, across the world, over 11 million young people between the ages of 15 and 24 had HIV/AIDS, and around half of all new infections happened in this group. In the majority of these cases the virus had been passed through heterosexual (male/female) sex without a condom, although in some areas intravenous drug abuse was also a big issue.

The reason that so many young people are being infected appears to be linked to the fact that they are more likely to experiment and have multiple sexual partners at this age, and are less likely to practise safe sex. In 2001, a study in the USA found that 61 per cent of teenagers said that they had had sex before graduating from high school, many taking no precautions at all. In many cases sexual activity takes place at a time when a lot of alcohol has been drunk, which makes it more likely that risks will be taken. Peer pressure is often an important factor – a young person may feel under pressure to be sexually active, like his or her friends.

But young people have also shown that they are able to act responsibly and look after their own health, if they have the right information. Sometimes, even when they are given the right information, they still take risks, perhaps because they lack self-confidence or they believe 'it can't happen to them'. Nevertheless, many government organizations and charities are working hard to give young people the facts they need to understand the risks and keep themselves safe.

High alcohol intake and illegal drug abuse at parties and clubs, like this rave in Denmark, can lead to unsafe sexual activity.

CASE STUDY

Marianne was 17 when she found out she was infected with HIV. She and her boyfriend, Sam, had known each other for 11 years. Marianne thought she knew everything there was to know about him.

Then one day the doctor called her in to his office and dropped the bombshell that she was HIV positive. Marianne was shocked. She remembers, 'I told Sam and he didn't believe me at first until he went and got tested and found out he was HIV positive too'. She later found out that, a year before, Sam had been drunk at a party and had slept with another girl who must have been carrying the virus.

Now Marianne has to take 23 tablets every day, but remains healthy. She and Sam are no longer together but are 'still best friends, and always will be'. Sadly, Sam's moment of irresponsibility has left a question mark over the future for both of them.

The HIV/AIDS Personal Stories website

Even being in a long-term relationship does not guarantee protection against HIV infection.

DEBATE

What should someone think about before they decide to be tested for HIV? If the test is positive, who should they tell?

4: HIV/AIDS in the Developing World

When AIDS first appeared over twenty years ago in the USA no one could have predicted that this was the beginning of an epidemic which would cause widespread death and destruction in many of the poorest countries of the world.

Today, the overwhelming majority of people with HIV infection, around 95 per cent, live in the developing world. At present, the countries of Africa are worst affected but HIV/AIDS is becoming more common in parts of Asia (especially India and China) and in some of the countries of the former Soviet Union in Eastern Europe. In these countries, which are already struggling to build a secure future for their people, HIV/AIDS is bringing huge challenges. Here we will focus on two of those areas of the world where HIV/AIDS is tightening its grip on the population – Africa and Eastern Europe.

A care supporter visits people living with AIDS in Zambia.

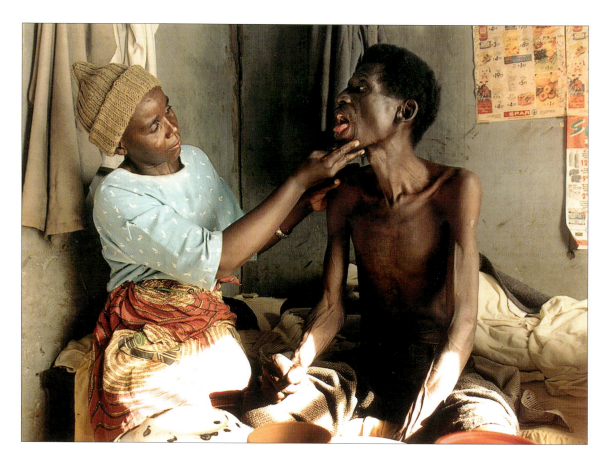

PERSPECTIVES

'AIDS today in Africa is claiming more lives than the sum total of all wars, famines and floods.'

Nelson Mandela, retired President of South Africa, quoted in New Internationalist magazine, June 2002

Why is HIV/AIDS more common in developing countries?

There are many reasons why HIV/AIDS is spreading so rapidly in developing countries. The powerful stigma associated with the disease causes difficulties in preventing and treating HIV/AIDS in these countries but another great problem is poverty. Many countries just do not have enough money to finance the type of healthcare needed to cope with the challenges of HIV/AIDS.

Preventing the spread of HIV/AIDS requires resources; money is needed to pay for public education campaigns and healthcare staff to teach people about the virus. And many people in developing countries do not have access to radio, television, newspapers or even schooling, from which they could learn about the risks of HIV/AIDS.

Inadequate healthcare may mean that if people become infected there are few doctors or hospitals to treat them. Many may never find out that they are infected with HIV and so pass it on to others unknowingly. Lack of money means that many people with HIV/AIDS in developing countries do not receive anti-HIV medicines, which are expensive.

Poverty and HIV/AIDS can form a vicious circle. If a country is poor, its people are more likely to catch HIV and eventually die (especially as they may already be weakened by malnutrition and illness before they become infected). Vulnerable groups, such as migrant workers and prostitutes, spread the disease particularly quickly, until it affects the whole of society. In Zimbabwe, for instance, AIDS has reduced average life expectancy from 65 to 39 years.

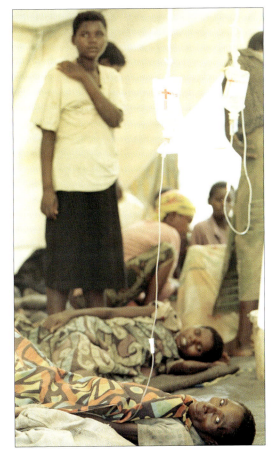

In the Democratic Republic of the Congo, years of war have made other problems, such as lack of food, water and healthcare, even worse. Here, refugees lie on the floor of a makeshift hospital tent.

As more people die, the workforce shrinks and the country becomes even poorer. One example of this is the way that HIV/AIDS is affecting the schooling of children in countries such as Malawi in Africa. Up to half the teachers in Malawi are expected to die of AIDS in the next five to seven years, leaving many children without any education and so little hope of getting good jobs to support themselves and their families in the future.

The role of women

In some developing countries, especially in Africa, women are becoming increasingly affected by HIV/AIDS. In 2002, a study in South Africa found that one in six women between the ages of 15 and 49 was infected with HIV, compared with only one in eight men. One reason for this is that in many traditional societies the status of women is very low and the men make all the important decisions. This may mean that women are not in a position to refuse to have sex or reduce their risk of catching HIV.

A nurse at a Salvation Army centre in Johannesburg, South Africa, feeds an HIV-infected baby who has been given up for adoption.

To make matters worse, when a woman becomes infected with HIV, often through her husband, she may be cast out of the family in disgrace.

As more and more women become infected with HIV, an increasing number of babies will be born with the infection. This is already a huge problem in parts of Africa, which has the highest number of HIV infected children in the world.

HIV/AIDS in Africa

The vast majority of people in the world who are infected with HIV/AIDS live in Africa. In 2001, over 28 million people in Africa carried the virus, and 2 million died of AIDS. The continent of Africa is made up of many different countries and each has its own pattern of HIV/AIDS infection. Some countries, especially in the north and west of the continent, are not too badly affected, but others have been devastated by the virus. In some countries in the south of the continent more than one in five adults is infected. In Botswana, more than one in three adults has HIV/AIDS.

The disease is putting an enormous strain on the economies of these countries, affecting healthcare, industry and education. Because many people cannot afford to pay for treatment, most of the people infected with HIV will develop AIDS and die. Millions of children are being left without parents, hospitals are losing their doctors and nurses, schools are going without teachers, and production of food and other goods is falling because workers are becoming sick. The situation is very serious.

CASE STUDY

Prisca is 41, and lives in the city of Harare, in Zimbabwe, a country in Africa with very high rates of HIV infection. She has tested positive for HIV.

Prisca knew that she must have caught the infection from her husband, who was a soldier. The hardest thing for her was that she was not allowed to tell anyone, 'My husband wanted me to keep it a secret and so, over the next few years, I lived a life full of lies,' she says.

When her husband died of AIDS a few years later his family blamed her and took all her possessions away, leaving her with just two remaining children. It was a difficult time.

But Prisca was determined to do what she could to fight HIV/AIDS. She joined the Network of Zimbabwean Positive Women and began to talk to others in her community about the condition. Although some people have treated her badly for this she will not give up. 'While AIDS continues to destroy my people, nothing will stop me talking about it,' says Prisca.

(Source: Actionaid's website. Interview 2001)

HIV/AIDS in Russia and Eastern Europe

HIV/AIDS is becoming a problem in Russia and parts of Eastern Europe. Since the fall of the Soviet Union at the end of the 1980s, it has become more possible for people from this part of the world to travel, and government control of people's behaviour has lessened. This has led to an increase in HIV/AIDS, especially among intravenous drug users. Outbreaks of HIV/AIDS among drug users were first reported in 1995 in the Ukraine. Since then, there have been more reports from many different areas of the former Soviet Bloc.

International monitoring organizations, such as the World Health Organization (WHO), have said that HIV/AIDS is growing faster in this region than anywhere else in the world. They have estimated that a million people in this area were affected by HIV/AIDS in 2001, a number which is expected to rise steeply every year. Most of these cases are among drug users but, as time goes on, others will probably also be affected.

The situation is made worse by the poor state of the healthcare system in Russia and Eastern Europe and the failure of the governments in these areas to accept the extent of the HIV/AIDS problem.

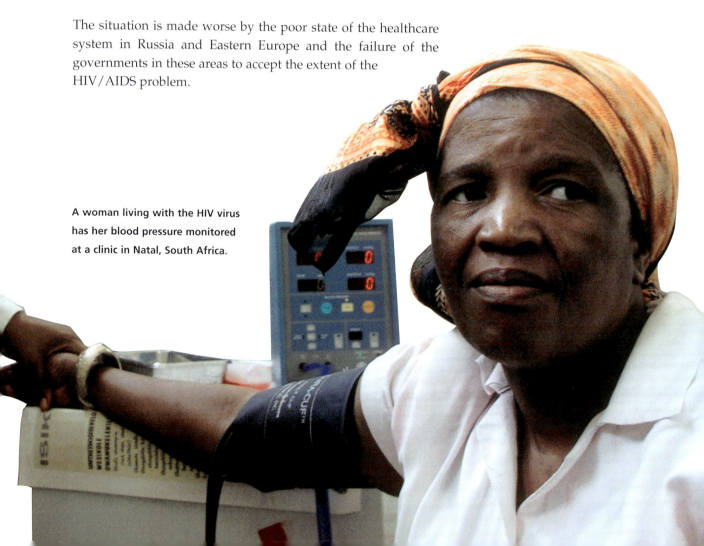

A woman living with the HIV virus has her blood pressure monitored at a clinic in Natal, South Africa.

CASE STUDY

Sergei used to be an intravenous drug user. Like many other drug users in Russia, this 24-year-old became HIV positive through the sharing of needles. But, unusually for someone in his community, Sergei decided to tell people he was infected. 'I'm not ashamed,' he says. 'I have the virus and I want to stop as many people as I can from sharing the same fate.'

Life can be very hard and unfair for those with HIV/AIDS in Russia. Sergei has found that the hospitals do not want to treat him because he carries the virus. There is little or no care available for those who are dying of AIDS.

Determined to help, Sergei joined a charity which works in the poorest parts of Moscow. He talks to young drug abusers, explaining to them the risks of HIV. Although there is not much money for their group Sergei works hard, saying, 'We don't have a lot of resources but we can help them fight their fear.'

(Source: New Internationalist magazine, June 2002. Article written by Olivia Ward)

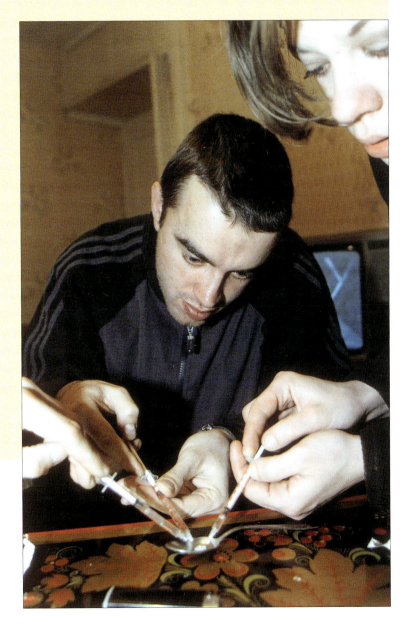

Young drug-users fill their syringes with heroin at an apartment in Moscow, Russia.

Access to anti-HIV medicines

People with HIV/AIDS in developed countries, such as the USA and the UK, usually have access to a range of anti-HIV medicines. These medicines, although they do not provide a cure, may allow the person to live healthily and even continue working for many years. Sadly, this is not the case for many people in the developing world. Anti-HIV medicines are very expensive and most people in poorer countries, such as those in Africa, simply do not have enough money to be able to buy them. For instance, even the cheapest anti-AIDS medicine costs over $300 a year, while the average health spending per person in Africa is only $5-10 a year.

This issue of the cost of anti-HIV medicines has become very controversial, causing arguments across the world. The pharmaceutical companies that make the medicines say they need to charge a lot for them because they were so expensive to develop and research. Meanwhile, campaigners say that no one should be prevented from getting the anti-HIV medicines they need. This disease is just too serious.

After receiving much criticism, some pharmaceutical companies have drastically cut the price of their anti-HIV medicines for the poorest countries. However, even these discounted prices are still too high for many people. To reduce the cost even further, some countries – such as Brazil and India – have decided to make their own, much cheaper copies of anti-HIV medicines. The big pharmaceutical companies claim that this is unfair. They say that these countries are stealing their ideas and taking advantage of all the research they have done.

GlaxoSmithKline

Logo for GlaxoSmithKline, which halved the cost of its anti-HIV medicines in 2003.

Many campaigners say that poor countries should be allowed to buy these cheap, copied anti-HIV medicines, and in some cases

PERSPECTIVES

'The price of anti-retrovirals [anti-HIV medicines] is a constant worry where the treatment of our people is concerned.'

Minister of Health Alain Yoda, from Burkina Faso, a poor country in Africa (Source: allAfrica.com website, April 2003)

Protesters call for more to be done to fight HIV/AIDS.

this has happened already. Although international law seems to support the position of the big pharmaceutical companies, campaigners say that HIV/AIDS is a health crisis where special rules should apply.

While all the arguments continue, many international and charitable organizations are trying to help the poorest countries buy anti-HIV medicines for their people. But the reality is that most people in these countries will never be given the chance to have the treatment they need and so will die unnecessarily.

DEBATE

Should poor countries be allowed to buy cheap, copied anti-HIV medicines for their people? Do you think this will affect the development of new medicines?

5: Looking to the Future

Scientists and doctors in research laboratories and hospitals around the world have been actively studying the virus for many years now, in an effort to understand how HIV spreads and causes disease in humans. The aims of this research are:

- to find better ways of preventing the spread of HIV/AIDS
- to discover more effective medicines to treat it
- and to develop a vaccine.

Over the years, scientists have found out a lot about the virus itself. They understand its structure, how it infects people, and how it causes damage to the immune system. However, further research into HIV, and especially its genetic make-up, is still needed in order to find better ways of preventing and treating infection.

Huge steps have been taken in treating HIV/AIDS. The large commercial pharmaceutical companies have invested a great deal of time and money in developing new medicines which have helped those people with HIV/AIDS who can afford them.

Kenyan scientist and AIDS researcher, Dr Julius Oyugi, prepares blood samples.

Every year, new anti-HIV medicines are brought out, each with some advantage over the previous ones. This research will no doubt continue until there is a medicine for HIV/AIDS that is really safe and effective.

A vaccine for HIV/AIDS?

However, although medicines for HIV/AIDS can prolong life, they cannot prevent the condition. What is needed is a vaccine. A vaccine triggers the body's immune system so that it can fight off an infection before it takes hold. And, unlike medicine, it does not have to be given again and again.

If an effective vaccine could be found, it would have an enormous impact on the worldwide HIV/AIDS epidemic. Many poor countries cannot afford anti-HIV medicines but, with help, they could probably afford vaccines for their populations. Millions of lives would be saved.

Many scientists, all over the world, are working hard to develop a vaccine for HIV/AIDS but it is proving very difficult. One of the problems is that the virus is so good at mutating – or changing its shape. Over time, this makes it harder to attack.

In February 2003, the results of the first trial of an HIV/AIDS vaccine were announced. They were very disappointing. Other trials for different vaccines are continuing in countries such as Thailand, Uganda and India, and it is hoped that one of these will have more promising results. But it does seem as though a vaccine against HIV/AIDS is still a long way off.

Mothers queue up at a rural health centre in Bangladesh to get their children vaccinated against polio. Maybe, one day, there will be a vaccine for AIDS like the one being given here.

PERSPECTIVES

'The problem of a vaccine is not impossible, just extremely difficult.'

Dr John Moore, Cornell University, USA.
(*Source:* Scientific American *website, May 2002*)

Not all bad news

There is no doubt that the world is in the middle of a serious epidemic of HIV/AIDS. However, there have been some success stories.

In many countries the government and media campaigns which told people of the risks of HIV/AIDS in the 1980s and 1990s did work. People began to change their behaviour so that they were less likely to catch HIV. Rates of infection in many countries levelled off and even began to fall. This shows that educating people about HIV/AIDS is a very effective way to fight the disease, though condoms also need to be made available cheaply and easily. Unfortunately, as time went by and HIV/AIDS was no longer so much in the news, many people seemed to forget about it and infection rates are now rising again.

But not all successes have been in the richer countries of the world. Many developing countries have taken the threat of HIV/AIDS seriously. One example is Brazil, which has encouraged its pharmaceutical companies to make cheaper anti-HIV medicines for its own people. And, by teaching about safe sex, Thailand, in the Far East, has managed to reduce the number of its people newly infected with HIV from a high of 140,000 a year to only 8,000.

In 2003, US President George W. Bush visited The AIDS Support Organization (TASO) in Uganda. Here, President Bush listens as Ugandan President Yoweri Museveni talks beside the orphaned children of Ugandan parents who have died of AIDS. TASO provides medical services to 30,000 people in Uganda each year.

Success in Uganda

Uganda is a large country in East Africa, home to over 25 million people. AIDS was recognized very early in Uganda – the first cases were seen in 1982. Ten years later, 1.5 million people in the country were infected with HIV/AIDS, one of the highest rates in the world at that time.

But today Uganda is one of the few countries in the developing world where the rates of HIV infection are actually falling. Possibly the most important factor is the attitude of the president, Yoweri Museveni. Instead of ignoring the disease as many other leaders had done, President Museveni spoke out about HIV/AIDS and called for international help to fight the epidemic within his population. In 1987, the Ugandan AIDS control programme launched a strong prevention and education campaign, and only a few years later the HIV infection rate began to fall. In the early 1990s, 14 per cent of the population was infected; this fell to only 8 per cent by the year 2000.

But why has Uganda been so successful when many similar countries have not? The answer may partly lie in the way the ordinary people of Uganda have responded to the challenge of HIV/AIDS. Instead of hiding from the truth, many people, including those with HIV/AIDS themselves, have formed community groups to educate people about the condition and support those who have it.

Crowds attend AIDS vigil on World AIDS Day.

Working together to fight HIV/AIDS

HIV/AIDS can only be fought effectively when people accept the facts about this condition and work together to stop it spreading. Everyone has a responsibility to learn about HIV/AIDS and take steps to keep themselves and others safe. Knowing the facts about HIV/AIDS (especially about how it is spread) should help to reduce the fear and stigma surrounding it. And this change in attitude will be a great help in ending the epidemic.

International co-operation

The problem of HIV/AIDS is too big for many countries to cope with on their own, especially the countries of the developing world. International co-operation is needed so that information and resources can be shared. For instance, scientific communities across the world share their knowledge about HIV/AIDS and co-operate in research, as in recent studies of new vaccines.

Charities, such as Actionaid and Médecins sans Frontières, raise money and set up projects to fight HIV/AIDS in many different countries. And, in 2002, the Global Fund to Fight AIDS, Tuberculosis and Malaria was set up by the United Nations. This international organization collects money from governments and businesses around the world to fight three diseases which are causing so many deaths today. However, as the promised funds have still not been committed by the wealthier countries, some people fear that it will not make much difference.

In 1988, the Director General of the World Health Organization announced the first World AIDS Day. Every year, on 1 December, events, press announcements and speeches are used to raise awareness of HIV/AIDS and the effect it is having around the world.

The challenge of HIV/AIDS

HIV is fast becoming one of the most destructive diseases that mankind has ever faced. The infection that seemed to begin as an outbreak among a small number of men in the United States

The Red Ribbon is the international symbol of AIDS awareness; a symbol of respect for those who have died of AIDS, of concern for those living with it, and a reminder to us all of the constant need to keep up the fight against AIDS. (From the World AIDS Day website)

CASE STUDY

Over the years HIV/AIDS has become a political issue, with many different activist organizations around the world working to ensure that the right decisions are taken by their governments.

One such group is AIDS Action, based in Washington DC in the USA. In 1984, some community groups who were looking after people with AIDS decided it was time to speak out; they felt that their political leaders were not doing enough to combat the epidemic. What was needed was '...a compelling voice of authority, compassion, and reason to engage and motivate our elected officials and our nation ... that voice would be AIDS Action.'

(Source: AIDS Action website)

has, in two decades, caused the death of millions of people across the globe.

While science can contribute towards the control of the virus, many people think that the best way to fight HIV/AIDS is through education. The virus spreads where there is fear and ignorance, where people are too embarrassed or too frightened to talk openly about the behaviour which can lead to infection. Much of the work of governments, health departments and AIDS charities is aimed at giving people, especially young people, the information they need to keep themselves safe.

Half of all new cases of HIV infection are now in young people under 25. If young people everywhere understood the facts about HIV/AIDS, the virus would begin to lose its grip. Then, one day, HIV/AIDS might finally become a thing of the past.

Secondary school pupils learning about HIV and AIDS. Education is a key factor in winning the battle.

DEBATE

What can young people do today to help in the fight against HIV/AIDS?

Glossary

antibodies defence chemicals made by the body to help fight off invading micro-organisms.

antivirals medicines which kill viruses.

asymptomatic having no symptoms; a disease which is asymptomatic may go unnoticed.

blood product a treatment made from human blood.

blood transfusion giving a person blood from another person.

condom also known as a 'rubber' or a 'sheath', this is a disposable latex sleeve which goes over the penis during sex. It stops HIV being passed on and also prevents pregnancy.

controversy a subject about which people disagree.

counsellor a person who is trained to listen and help people cope with their problems.

developed countries countries, such as the USA, UK, Australia, and those in Western Europe, with a high standard of living and modern industries.

developing countries countries that are still trying to achieve a more 'modern' way of life. Sometimes also known as 'Third World' countries, these are in parts of Africa, the Indian subcontinent and South-East Asia.

discrimination treating people unfairly based on issues such as race, gender, disability or age.

Factor VIII (factor 8) the blood product used to treat the condition haemophilia.

gay a word often used to describe someone who is homosexual.

haemophilia a genetic blood disorder, present from birth, where the blood does not clot properly.

heterosexual being sexually attracted to people of the opposite sex.

high-risk activities behaviour which carries an increased chance of passing on or catching HIV. The most common high-risk activities are sex without a condom and sharing dirty needles.

HIV positive infected with the HIV virus, as shown by a blood test. This is not the same as having AIDS.

HIV test a blood test which looks for antibodies to HIV.

homosexual being sexually attracted to people of the same sex.

immune system the body's defences against invading micro-organisms such as viruses.

intravenous drugs medicines or illegal drugs which are injected directly into a vein.

Kaposi's sarcoma an unusual type of skin cancer which may occur in AIDS.

life expectancy the number of years a person can expect to live.

pharmaceutical company commercial organization which researches new medicines and then sells them at a profit.

pneumocystis pneumonia a rare type of lung disease which may occur in AIDS.

protease a chemical which HIV uses to make new copies of itself.

reverse transcriptase a chemical which HIV uses to make new copies of itself.

safe sex sexual activities which avoid the exchange of body fluids which might contain HIV.

semen the fluid passed from the man to the woman during sex.

stigma shame, fear and embarrassment.

T-cells the blood cells which are the target of the viruses in HIV infection.

United Nations an organization made up of representatives of nearly all the countries of the world. It works for international peace and economic stability.

vaccine a special medicine that is given, usually by injection, to a healthy person in order to prevent them catching a particular infectious disease in the future.

vaginal secretions the fluid made by the walls of the vagina. It may come into contact with the penis during sex.

virus a very tiny micro-organism which can infect someone.

window period the period of time between someone catching HIV and developing enough antibodies to give a positive blood test. The test appears negative but the virus can still be passed on.

Useful Addresses

www.aegis.com
AEGiS (AIDS Education Global Information System)
A web-based database of information about HIV/AIDS.

www.unaids.org
UNAIDS (The Joint United Nations Programme on HIV/AIDS)
This organization was formed in 1996 to co-ordinate efforts to fight HIV/AIDS across the world.

www.thebody.com
The Body
The Body is a respected American organization which runs a website with a wide range of information about all aspects of HIV/AIDS.

www.hivinsite.ucsf.edu
HIV Insite
Comprehensive, up-to-date information on HIV/AIDS treatment, prevention and policy from the University of California, San Francisco.

www.whatudo.org
HIV Insite's teenage website
This website for young people carries straightforward and readable information about HIV/AIDS.

www.avert.org
AVERT
AVERT is an international HIV/AIDS charity based in the UK, which aims to help prevent the spread of HIV/AIDS worldwide.

www.tht.org.uk
Terrence Higgins Trust
The Terrence Higgins Trust is one of the leading HIV/AIDS charities in the UK. Their website carries details of their groups around the country.

www.actionaid.org
Actionaid
As one of the UK's largest development agencies, Actionaid works in more than 30 countries in Africa, Asia, Latin America and the Caribbean.

Further Reading

Understanding HIV and Aids
(The Terrence Higgins Trust, available from their website)
This readable booklet provides general information about HIV and AIDS. It explains what HIV and AIDS are, and how HIV can be transmitted. It also covers the facts about HIV testing, looks at how HIV affects the body, and includes a useful chapter on where to get support and further information.

The following books are all written with teenagers in mind:

Need To Know – AIDS
Sean Connolly
(Heinemann Library, 2002)

AIDS
Jo Whelan
(Hodder Wayland, Health Issue Series, 2001)

AIDS and HIV: Risky Business
Daniel Jussim
(Enslow Publishers Inc, 1997)

Everything you need to know about AIDS and HIV (Need to Know Library)
(Rosen Publishing Group, 2001)

AIDS, a handbook for the future
Marianne Le Vert
(Millbrook Productions, 1996)

AIDS (Diseases and People)
Janet Majure
(Enslow Publishers Inc., 1998)